English Version [illegible] Published in November 2013

Photography by Jessica Hayes

Maps by Jessica Hayes

Email: jessicahayes@eurotourguide.com

Web: www.eurotourguide.com

ISBN 978-84-937438-1-9

Intellectual Property Register Deposito Legal A-584-2013

Printed by Publidisa

Map of Days Out

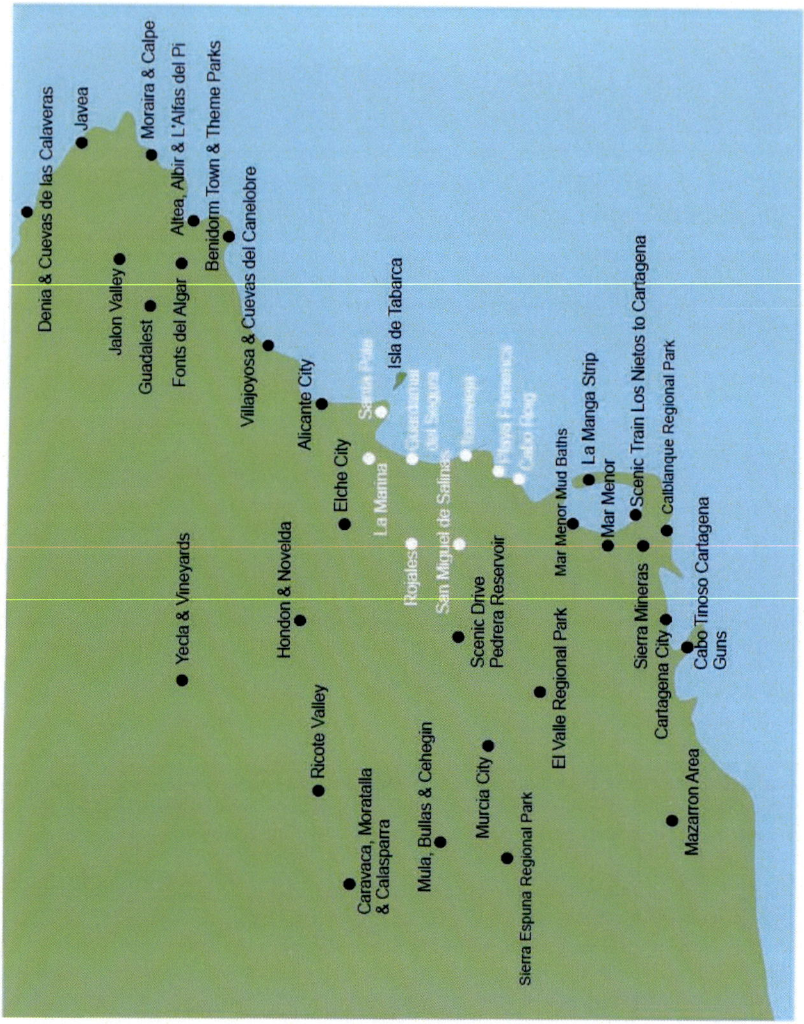

Contents and Journey Times

Times in minutes from starting towns to first co-ordinate using tolls roads and the fastest route as provided by a mapping website.

Day Out Fonts del Algar	22-23	99	90	84	0
Day Out Benidorm Theme Parks	24	76	67	61	57
Day Out Guadalest	25-27	104	92	85	82
Day Out Hondon and Novelda (via Albertera)	28-29	61	53	46	52
Day Out Isla de Tabarca (Santa Pola Marina)	30-31	48	43	30	18
Day Out Jalon Valley	32-33	98	90	83	79
Day Out Javea	34-35	109	100	94	90
Day Out La Manga Strip	36-37	53	50	60	69
Day Out Mar Menor	38-39	32	30	39	48
Day Out Mar Menor Mud Baths	40-41	20	18	27	36
Day Out Mazarron Area	42-43	59	57	66	71
Day Out Mula, Bullas and Cehegin	44-45	65	63	63	69
Day Out Ricote Valley	46-47	75	70	62	68
Scenic Train Journey Los Nietos to Cartagena	48-49	43	40	50	59
Day Out Sierra Mineras	50-51	42	40	49	58
Day Out Villajoyosa and Cuevas del Canelobre	52-53	75	66	60	55

Links to Website

When you see this symbol take a look at the related Days Out Travel Guide on the website www.eurotourguide.com for more information including open times, prices and links to the official website.

Day Out Altea, Albir and L'Alfas del Pi

A visit to the towns of Altea and Albir, the coastal part of L'Alfas del Pi, makes for a great day out. They are situated just a few kilometres apart and are a perfect contrast to each other. In Altea it's all about the old town and in Albir it is all about the beach!

Altea is without doubt one of the most charming towns of the Costa Blanca North. It's old town is packed full of character and the impressive church with it's blue and white tiled dome roof has to be one of the most photographed landmarks of the area. It's cobbled lanes, many of which are stepped, wind up to the plaza at the top of the hill with the church and magnificent views of the mountains and the sea. The pedestrianised streets are packed with top class restaurants and a fascinating array of tiny shops offering exquisite local crafts, paintings and gifts.

L'Alfas del Pi is a town of two halves; the original fortified village which is located some 4 kilometres inland and the much more recent sea-side village known as Albir (as we'll call it from now on). Albir has a beautiful sandy beach and an attractive palm fringed promenade called Paseo de las Estrellas (Stars' Promenade) in honour of the famous actors and actresses who have scooped awards at the International Film Festival that L'Alfas del Pi hosts every July.

Altea Old Town Car Park **N38°35.930 W0°03.358**

There are other car parks in Altea, but by parking in this one you avoid the steep walk up to the old town. Just cross the road and walk along any of the streets following the signs for the Poble Antic for the old town.

Altea Beach & Marina Car Park **N38°35.835 W0°02.975**

Turn left or right for the beach and promenade with a selection of restaurants or cross the road and walk up into the old town.

Albir Beach Car Park N38°34.420 W0°03.948

Walk down to the sandy beach and promenade or follow the road uphill for shops and restaurants.

Albir Lighthouse Car Park N38°34.094 W0°03.814

Parking is in the car park and is free. Follow the old road and signs along the cliff to the lighthouse about 5 kilometres away.

Day Out Benidorm Town

The Costa Blanca's tourist capital and the Mediterranean equivalent of New York! Like it or dislike it, Benidorm is a must see for everyone, even if it is just so that you can say 'I've been there'!

Over recent years Benidorm has been transformed into a major tourist destination. It has two wonderful promenades to choose from along Poniente and Levante beach as well as a small marina. The bustling, historic old quarter is well worth a visit and in particular the three plazas of Santa Ana, Castelar and Castell from which there are breathtaking views of both beaches and the impressive skyline. Just behind this, is a thriving shopping area with all of the major brands and high street names, as well as a wealth of bars, cafes and restaurants. Add to this the street market, the lively nightly entertainment and the four theme parks, there is so much to see and do here that you'll want to return again and again.

Benidorm Car Park **N38°32.333 W0°07.733**

Parking is in the underground car park and is charged for by the length of stay. Exit the car park and walk back along the same road that you've just driven along, go straight on at the roundabout with the anchor on it and under the bridge to the Plaza de Hispanidad, then head down to the Levante beach. Once at the beach looking out to sea turn right for the old town, marina and Poniente beach.

There are various boat trips available from the marina, including one to visit Dove or Peacock Island in the middle of the bay.

Benidorm Large Market **N38°32.425 W0°06.745**

Parking is anywhere you can find a space, check carefully as not all parking is free, alternatively park in the underground car park and walk. Market days are Sunday and Wednesday mornings.

AQUARIO II
MUNDO-SUBMARINO

Day Out Moraira and Calpe

A trip to the seaside towns of Moraira and Calpe in the Costa Blanca North makes for a great day out. It gives a true taste of what the area has to offer and the scenic drive from Calpe to Moraira is stunning. It is the restaurants which keep people returning to both of these places time and time again, as they enjoy quality fresh fish straight out of the sea!

The tranquil town of Moraira remains the most unspoilt coastal town of the area. Moraira has an exclusive affluent feel to it which is confirmed by the little 'castle' on the sea front. The small marina, the promenades, viewpoints and small shopping district along with the 8 kilometres of blue flag beaches, some sandy and some rocky, add to the charm of this seaside resort.

Calpe, also spelt without the 'e' as Calp, is instantly recognised by the mighty Penon de Ifach, the huge rock which rises 332 meters out of the Mediterranean sea. The Rock of Ifach was declared a nature reserve in 1987 and now provides a safe haven for a variety of birds and unusual flora and fauna. There are quality sandy beaches, kilometres of sea front promenades, excellent local shopping facilities including a large Saturday morning street market and a wealth of bars and restaurants offering all kinds of cuisine.

Moraira Beach North End **N38°41.303 E0°08.758**

Platja del Portet, the car park and is free but be careful as it floods.

Moraira Central Car Park **N38°41.344 E0°07.911**

This car park is closed on Fridays as it is the site of the market.

Moraira Beach South End **N38°41.148 E0°07.561**

Platja de Platgetes, parking in the car park or any space along the road.

Moraira Scenic Drive to Calpe **N38°40.875 E0°07.095**

Calpe Scenic Driving to Moraira **N38°38.560 E0°04.089**

Follow along the CV746 between these two start / finish points.

Calpe Beach North End **N38°38.554 E0°04.330**

Playa Levante, park in the marked spaces along the road.

Calpe Parque Natural Penon de Ifach N38°38.347 E0°04.352

Park in the car park and follow the path through the rock!

Calpe Beach South End **N38°38.545 E0°03.024**

Playa L'Arenal-Bol, there are lots of paying car parks, choose one.

Day Out Denia and Cuevas de las Calaveras

A visit to the castle at Denia followed by an afternoon at the nearby Cuevas de las Calaveras is a great actioned packed day out.

Denia enjoys a privilege position right on the northern edge of the province of Alicante. It sits on the shores of the Mediterranean opposite the Balearic Islands and is backed by the impressive mountains of the the Montgo Natural park. Denia is packed with many places of interest. A coffee in the old town or along the impressive tree lined main street is a good idea, before heading up to the castle ruins. The castle proudly guards the town and is great fun to explore. Most of the buildings which used to occupy the grounds have long gone, leaving a big open space behind the imposing castle walls. Within the castle is a museum which explains the history of Denia, but it is the views from the very top of the castle out over the sea that are simply amazing.

The Cuevas de las Calaveras are located just 15 kilometres inland along the road between Pedreguer and Benidoleig. The caves got their rather sinister name, the Caves of the Skulls, from the many skulls that were found in them when they were discovered in 1768. There is an interesting historical display which outlines the formation of the cave system and details some of its subsequent uses. During WWII soldiers used the cave to store food and even to repair aircraft engines!

Denia Car Park **N38°50.819 E0°06.522**

Parking is in any of the spaces beside the road or in the large gravelled car park and is free, walk through the old town to the castle and main tree lined high street.

Denia Castle **N38°50.496 E0°06.346**

You'll need to park in the car park and walk up to the castle. This is the coordinate for the castle entrance or you can just follow the signs to the Centre Historic and the Castillo.

🔗 For the most up to date information about opening times and prices take a look at the official link on the website.

Cuevas de las Calaveras **N38°47.596 W0°01.078**

Parking is in the car park and is free. It can be cold inside the caves, so make sure you bring some warm clothes.

🔗For the most up to date information about opening times and prices take a look at the official link on the website.

Day Out Cabo Tinoso Cartagena Guns

After a stop at the marina in the City of Cartagena, enjoy the scenic drive south towards Mazarron. You'll wind your way along the valley floor and then, after a steep ascent arrive at the top of the Cabo Tinoso mountain.

Here you'll find abandoned buildings which look almost castle like and two massive Vickers guns (38.1 centimetre 1926 models). They were constructed between 1926 and 1933 as part of an ambitious network of coastal defensive designed to protect the military base or Arsenal in Cartagena. More information about them can be found in the Cartagena Military Museum. The guns were apparently last fired on the 26th April 1973 by Republicans at a group of Nationalist cruisers. In such a tranquil setting it is hard to imagine the boom that the guns would have made as their artillery travelled the 20 miles to its target.

There are several things to be aware of. The road, in some places is very twisty and narrow with steep drops to one side so you must be a confident driver. There are no facilities of any kind at the guns, so bring a picnic with you. Make sure you wear good shoes for walking over rough ground and if you want to explore the underground tunnels (all at your own risk) then bring a torch.

To finish your day out in style, travel on to the Port of Mazarron, for a stroll beside the marina!

Cartagena City Centre **N37°35.876 W0°59.052**

Parking is in the underground car park beside the marina and is charged for by length of stay. Exit the car park onto the promenade, the marina and a selection of cafes are right in front of you.

Cabo Tinoso Cartagena Guns **N37°32.394 W1°07.133**

Parking is anywhere you please and is free, the complex is made up of several different areas, so you might like to drive between the 'bases'. There are many areas to explore, so just enjoy! Don't forget to wear good shoes, bring a torch and pack a picnic and remember there are no facilities of any kind here.

Mazarron Coastal Town **N37°33.880 W1°15.508**

Parking is in the underground car park and is charged for by the length of stay. Walk along past the boats of the marina for the cafes and bars.

Day Out Calblanque Regional Park

The Calblanque Regional Park, which has been a Protected Natural Area since 1987 and Nature Reserve since 1992 makes for a great day out. It covers an area of 2400 hectares and has 13 kilometres of coastline. Within its boundaries is an awe inspiring collection of wonderful sand beaches, sandbanks, arid hills, cliff tops and salt flats all of great ecological value.

This Nature Reserve represents one of the last untouched areas along the Mediterranean coastline and is truly unspoilt. There are no facilities here (apart from some toilets at the visitors centre) so don't forget to pack a picnic! Please be aware that the undercurrents are strong in this area as the bottom of the sea drops steeply away in line with the cliffs above.

Finish your day out in style with a stop in nearby Cabo de Palos at the marina or the light house.

Park Entrance **N37°37.366 W0°45.184**

This isn't an actual stop, but the best entrance point for the Calblanque Regional Park, drive along the dirt track (your sat nav might warn you that the roads are unpaved) with fields on either side to all the destinations in the park.

Visitors Centre **N37°36.619 W0°45.466**

Parking is in the car park and is free. There is information about the fauna, flora and geology of the park as well as leaflets and notice boards which show the routes.

Beach Playa Calblanque **N37°36.232 W0°43.935**

Beach Playa Negrete **N37°35.975 W0°45.552**

Cabo de Palos Lighthouse **N37°38.020 W0°41.466**

Parking is in the car park and is free, alternatively you can park near the marina and walk!

Cabo de Palos Marina **N37°37.989 W0°42.100**

Parking is on the street beside the marina. Walk past the boats to the restaurants which are found along the seafront at the mouth of the marina. For the beach, cross the road and take any of the streets between the houses.

Day Out El Valle Regional Park

The Regional Park of El Valle and Carrascoy is located about 6 kilometres to the east of the city of Murcia and is nicked named the 'green lung' of Murcia. It covers an area of 11,000 hectares and its mountains range from 200 to 1,000 metres in height. It has been a protected area since 1917 and was declared a regional park in 1992.

There is an abundance of fauna and flora. Such animals as the natterjack toad, montpellier snake, striped necked terrapin, red squirrels, wild boar, sparrow hawks and golden eagles inhabit the park. There are more than 600 species of plants; including aleppo pine, evergreen oak, rosemary, thyme, esparto grass and oleanders.

The mountains of this area have been inhabited by hermits since the 5th century and the park has many religious buildings to visit like the impressive La Fuensanta Sanctuary. There are two free visitor centres, the Centro Naturaleza El Valle and the Centro de la Luz as well as a fascinating Arboretum. There is an abundance of signposted walking and cycling routes, a road to the top of El Relojeroat 609 metres and even barbecue facilities (winter only) and plenty of picnic tables positioned throughout the park.

La Fuensanta Sanctuary **N37°56.265 W1°07.056**

Parking is in the car park and is free. Put a 1€ coin into the slot machine to the right of the door in the church foyer to light up the dome. Visit at sunset for some spectacular views! There is also a little souvenir shop and cafe.

🔗For the most up to date information about opening times and prices take a look at the official link on the website.

Naturaleza Visitors Centre **N37°55.701 W1°08.419**

Parking and entrance is free, there are several interactive exhibitions about the fauna and flora. The centre is normally open Tuesday-Sunday 10:00-18:00.

Arboretum **N37°55.701 W1°08.419**

La Luz Visitors Centre **N37°55.974 W1°07.590**

It is free to park and visit. There is an information desk, with walking and cycling maps, exhibitions about the park, café, mountaineering exhibition and a 360 degree viewing balcony.

🔗For the most up to date information about opening times and prices take a look at the official link on the website.

San Antonio el Pobre Hermitage **N37°55.922 W1°07.936**

Parking is beside the entrance gates and is free, take care not to use the private parking spaces. In the little hermitage they will play a 10 minute video about the life of hermits in these mountains and is free to visit.

🔗For the most up to date information about opening times and prices take a look at the official link on the website.

Playground, BBQ & Picnic Areas **N37°55.636 W1°08.260**

Murcia City Car Park **N37°58.953 W1°07.755**

Parking is in the underground car park beside the river and is charged for by length of stay. Walk away from the river to enter the Cathedral Square and follow our City Walking Route.

Day Out Caravaca, Moratalla & Calasparra

The inland part of the province of Murcia is just as delightful and worth visiting as the coastal part. It has spectacular scenery as it lies within the Espuna and Revolcadores Mountains along the banks of the Segura river. There are many charming towns and villages that have been inhabited since prehistoric times, and plenty of unique culture as this area has remained relatively isolated through history.

This day out is designed to give you a good feel for the area, but there is so much to see and do in all three places that you might prefer to spend the whole day visiting only one of them. Or perhaps you can 'mix and match' these destinations with the villages of Mula, Bullas or Cehegin which you'll pass on the way to Caravaca.

Caravaca de la Cruz is of huge religious significance to all Catholics. It is ranked amongst the top five most religious places in the world alongside Rome and Jerusalem as it is said to have a fragment of the cross on which Jesus was crucified. Caravaca is a major tourist magnet with many things to see and do including several museums and religious buildings as well as a popular artists market which is held on the third Sunday of every month.

The old quarter of Moratalla is a delight to wander around with its quirky streets. The Castle Fortaleza, built in the 9th century provides an excellent view point.

Calasparra is famous for producing rice, you can learn more about it by visiting the Rice Museum and following the Rice Walking Route. It has a popular Artisan Market every second Sunday of each month in the Plaza de la Corredera and a visit to the Sanctuary of Our Lady of Hope beside the Rio Segura is a must.

Caravaca de la Cruz **N38°06.642 W1°51.804**

Parking is on the side of the road and is free, walk downhill following the river, at the bridge beside the Fiesta Museum turn right, the first building is the tourist office.

Moratalla N38°11.334 W1°53.434

Parking is in the street and is free. Walk uphill and turn right at the crossroads, continue along Calle Tomas El Cura into the old quarter.

Calasparra N38°13.906 W1°42.010

Parking is in the street and is free, continue along the street to the large junction, turn left and continue into the heart of the town.

Calasparra Viewpoint N38°15.387 W1°42.460

Calasparra Sanctuary N38°15.730 W1°42.673

Parking is in the car park and is free, walk through the gates to explore the sanctuary or through the car parks to get to the river.

Day Out Fonts del Algar

The Fonts del Algar or Fonts de L'Algar as it is also known is a series of naturally occurring waterfalls which are only 15km from Benidorm. They have become very popular in recent years and during the hot summer months are a tourist magnet.

For the most scenic route take the road which passes through the small village of Polop. Once at the waterfalls, follow the other tourists to either of the two entrances. After paying you can explore the river, waterfalls and pools at your leisure as they are open from morning until dusk. Walk along beside the river, swim (at your own risk) in the rock pools, dangle your feet in the flowing water, enjoy your picnic or find a quiet spot to sit under the pine trees. You can exit by following the path uphill behind the first aid station, this takes you to the arboretum, picnic area and museum of the environment. The museum houses various exhibits about the local flora and fauna as well as a gift shop! Further up the hill there is a botanical garden with over 500 different species of cactus and succulents.

For a full day and a scenic circular route make a visit to the historic mountain top village and castle of Guadalest.

Polop Village Centre **N38°37.386 W0°07.941**

Park on the waste ground and enjoy a morning coffee before heading towards the waterfalls.

Fonts del Algar **N38°39.500 W0°05.901**

Parking is in any of the private car parks which line the road prior to the entrance or in the public car park further along the road, there is a charge for all the car parks. There are two entrances to the waterfalls, both of which have ticket offices, one at the top and one at the bottom of the falls, use either entrance and enjoy! There is also a Museum of the Environment, Arboretum, picnic area and several restaurants some with swimming pools.

🔗 For the most up to date information about opening times and prices take a look at the official link on the website.

Cactus Garden **N38°39.162 W0°05.420**

The Cacturs Garden contains over 500 different species of cactus and succulents.

🔗For the most up to date information about opening times and prices take a look at the official link on the website.

Guadalest Car Park **N38°40.557 W0°12.006**

Entrance to the village with its craft and souvenir shops is free, but there is a charge for the car park and the castle ruins as well as the independent museums.

Day Out Benidorm Theme Parks

Benidorm has four theme parks. Keep a look out for discount vouchers which are often available in the papers, from supermarkets, via the web and if you buy your tickets in advance.

🔗For the most up to date information about opening times and prices take a look at the official link on the website.

Terra Mitica **N38°33.461 W0°09.382**

Terra Mitica has many heart pounding rides and spectacular shows all based around the five ancient civilisations of the Mediterranean. It has Pirates, Gladiators and Comedy performers to add to the fun and excitement! There is a fixed charge for parking in the car park.

Terra Natura & Aqua Natura **N38°34.165 W0°08.751**

At Terra Natura there are over 1,500 animals and 2,500 trees, bushes and plants. The park is themed around the continents of Asia, Europe and America as well as the 80 million years old volcanic landmass known as Pangea. Aqua Natura is the water park area of Terra Natura, it has over 800m of water slides, various pools and man-made white sandy beaches. There is a fixed charge for parking in the car park.

Mundomar & Aqualandia **N38°32.527 W0°05.696**

Mundomar is full of wonderful and exotic animals. There are lots of shows to watch such as the Dancing Dolphins, the Sea Lions or the Parrot displays and a children's adventure playground. Parking is in the car park and is free.

Aqualandia is the main water park. There are over 20 rides and areas all of which involve water. There are the fast and furious rapids, the long and steep kamikaze, the sedate and slowly flowing lazy river to name a few! Parking is in the car park and is free.

Day Out Guadalest

The historic hill fort of Guadalest is situated just 25km inland from the town of Benidorm. It is a major tourist attraction having been declared a 'Monument of Historical and Artistic Value' in 1974. It charms over 2 million visitors every year and is a truly spectacular sight – the remains of a medieval castle and village precariously perched on top of a mountain overlooking a reservoir.

Start your day with a morning coffee stop in Polop and then take the scenic route past the historic vehicles museum to Guadalest. For something different you can enjoy a trip on the solar powered boat that glides across the reservoir below Guadalest.

The impressive entrance to the fort and village of Guadalest is via a 15 metre long tunnel which has been carved through the solid rock. There are numerous interesting museums to visit as well as the castle ruins, all of which have entrance charges. There are lots of souvenir shops where you can spend several hours browsing the vast displays of trinkets and quality art work and various restaurants to choose from.

Travel back in time with a visit to Guadalest and enjoy its stunning mountain scenery, top quality craft shops, many museums and local restaurants.

Polop Village Centre **N38°37.386 W0°07.941**

Park on the waste ground and enjoy a morning coffee before heading towards the waterfalls.

Historic Vehicles Museum **N38°39.853 W0°09.653**

The museum contains over 100 motorcycles and several small cars from the 1920's to the 1970's.

🔗For the most up to date information about opening times and prices take a look at the official link on the website.

Guadalest Car Park **N38°40.557 W0°12.006**

Entrance to the village with its craft and souvenir shops is free, but there is a charge for the car park and museums; these include the:

- San Jose Castle.
- Casa Orduna, the house of the guardians of the castle and governors of the estate, it is set over four floors and is built into the rock face, the most interesting room is the library which houses 1265 books, 589 of which appear in the catalogue of the "Ancient Books" (1500–1800)!
- Salt & Pepper Pots Museum, displays over 20,000 salt and pepper pots from around the world, take a look at the website
- Dolls House Museum with many different dolls houses set over three floors.
- Ethnological Museum, shows how people lived, what tools and implements they used and the clothes that they wore.
- Microgigantic Museum, with the aid of magnifying glasses you can marvel at this miniature world and see such things as a flea riding a bicycle on the edge of a seed!
- Miniature Museum, another museum of miniature marvels such as the statue of Liberty within the eye of a needle!
- Medieval Torture Museum, barbaric medieval to almost present times instruments of torture and execution gathered from Europe.

🔗For the most up to date information about opening times and prices take a look at the official link on the website.

Reservoir & Solar Powered Boat **N38°40.713 W0°11.548**

Parking is free and is on the side of the road, follow the path through the trees to the jetty. The boat completes a 5km circuit in about 50min.

🔗For the most up to date information, timetables and prices take a look at the official link on the website.

MUSEO

LA TENDA

Day Out Hondon and Novelda

This day is all about the scenery of the mountains of Crevillente and the valley of the Hondons, as well as the spectacular sanctuary of Saint Mary Magdalene overlooking the Vinalope valley. It can be a very leisurely full day, an action packed half day or combined with a stop at the El Hondo Nature Park, a protected area for birds and wetland.

Past Albatera you travel through the fertile plains of the Vega Baja, to the start of the ascent over the Sierra de Crevillente which stand at a height of 838m. Slowly wind your way up and over the pass, admiring the stunning views. After driving through Hondon de los Frailes, the first stop is at Hondon de las Nieves. The name has nothing to do with snow but comes from the Virgen de las Nieves, the patron saint of the village. This is a picturesque Spanish mountain village, with lots of little tapas bars and restaurants for you to enjoy. There is also the local Bodega Cerda with its little museum and shop dedicated to everything to do with wine!

Onwards to Novelda, and the Sanctuary of Saint Mary Magdalene and castle of La Mola. This religious building was built by local Novelda based engineer Jose Sala Sala, with work beginning in 1918 and finishing in 1946. The outside is 100% more impressive than the inside. Next to the sanctuary is the castle of La Mola, built in the late 12th century. You can climb the 11m high tower for a true feel of the castle.

Albatera **N38°11.088 W0°52.327**

This isn't an actual stop, but a drive through so that you approach the Sierras de Crevillent along the correct road - the CV873, although you can park and explore if you wish.

Hondon de las Nieves **N38°18.526 W0°51.285**

Parking is on the road and is free. For the village centre walk straight on past the traffic lights and pharmacy, for the Bodega Cerda walk in the opposite direction, along the road you have just driven in on.

🔗 For the most up to date information about the bodega take a look at the official link on the website.

Novelda Sanctuary & Mola Castle **N38°24.519 W0°47.647**

Parking is in the car park and is free. The inside of the church and the castle can only be visited during opening hours, but you can wander around the outside at any time. Admire the architecture and views and enjoy the peace and tranquillity. If you want to climb up inside the castle (at your own risk) then remember to bring a torch!

🔗For the most up to date information about opening times and prices take a look at the official link on the website.

Day Out Isla de Tabarca

The tiny island of Tabarca is one of the top tourist destinations within the Costa Blanca. A visit here is just like stepping back in time, although it can feel quite crowded during the height of summer as over 4,000 people visit it daily! In 1986 the island and its waters were declared a protected marine and bird reserve.

Boats to Tabarca leave from Torrevieja, Guardamar, Alicante and Benidorm, although for the most frequent crossings, widest choice of boats and shortest journey of about half an hour, it is best to depart from Santa Pola's marina. Some boats have glass bottoms, so you can admire the creatures of the deep, whilst others operate as a taxi for parties as small as 6 people.

Once on the Island you can explore!! There is the old square at the heart of Tabarca, the church and graveyard, the museum, the ruined walls of the fort, the lighthouse, the beaches and coves, the paths that crisscross the island, an abundance of bars and restaurants as well as souvenir shops. If that isn't enough there is the crystal clear waters for some top class snorkelling!

Santa Pola Marina Car Park **N38°11.295 W0°33.619**

Parking is in the pay car park and is charged by the length of stay, keep your ticket and pay when you are ready to leave. Free parking is available on the roads around this area, but spaces can be very hard to find, especially during holiday times. Exit the car park to the right and walk along beside the boats towards the fishing fleet, the boats for Tabarca depart from here.

There are several companies which offer trips to and from the Island. The prices and timetables for the half hour journey for the big boats are displayed on the boards at the information hut. There are several independent 'taxi' boats which hold 6-10 people, negotiation with their captains is possible.

🔗For the most up to date information, timetables and prices take a look at the official link on the website.

Isla Tabarca **N38°10.597 W0°28.786**

Explore the Island, it is only 1750 metres long and 300 metres wide! There is the central village square, the old fort of which the walls and three of the gates houses still survive, the impressive church, the lighthouse which sits on the uninhabited tip of the island it keeps watch over the sea and a museum for information about the history of the island and its roll as a marine reserve. There are also several beaches and coves, some are completely covered in seaweed, others are pebbled and few of the larger ones have sunbeds and sun umbrellas for hire. The island offers great snorkelling, so remember your snorkel & flippers! There are a selection of bars, cafes and restaurants, they are slightly more expensive than usual so you might want bring your own picnic.

Day Out Jalon Valley

The Jalon Valley, also known as the Xalo Valley is situated in the Marina Alta area in the Costa Blanca North and is quite simply stunning. The Marina Alta has a delightful mix of coastline and mountains, but it is its inland area that provides the great setting for this amazingly scenic day out.

Gata de Gorgos, the first stop of the day, has a long tradition of wicker making and there are plenty of shops selling all things wicker from dog baskets to table mats and even light shades! Following the course of the river Jalon the scenery is the main attraction. Fields of almond, olive and citrus trees as well as vines border both sides of the road. If you're making this journey during February you're in for a treat as the almond blossom will be in full bloom!! The village of Jalon makes a great stop as there are a couple of bodegas where you can sample the local wines, or continue to Alcalali for a stretch of the legs and a taster of a traditional inland village. After this, the mountain climb begins up to the Coll de Rates. The 360 degree panoramic vistas from the top are amazing, on a clear day you can see Mallorca!! On the way down you'll pass through the village of Polop, another ideal stop for a wander and refreshment before heading home.

Gata de Gorgos Town Centre N38°46.549 E0°05.032

Parking is in any of the side streets off this main road and is free. Walk from here back along the main road and to the small Plaza de Espana, where the shop with lots of plates set into the wall is. You'll have passed some wicker shops and cafes, the rest of the small town is ahead of you, on the other side of the plaza.

Top tip: you'll be driving back to this Plaza de Espana and then along the narrow street off the the right to start your journey into the Jalon valley, so walk along it now, after a few hundred meters you'll see a small sign on the wall at the first road on your right that says Jalon / Xalo, you'll be turning right here in your car.

Jalon or Xalo Valley

This isn't a stop but the name of the valley, it is well known for its almond blossom, so if your making this journey during February you'll be in for a treat! Stop where you like to take photos.

Jalon or Xalo Village Centre **N38°44.547 W0°00.838**

Parking is on the side of the road and is free, it is best to avoid entering the village as the streets are narrow so try to park as close to the bodegas as possible. Head for the church spire to discover the streets of the village.

Alcalali Village Centre **N38°45.106 W0°02.466**

Parking is on the side of the road and is free, it is best to avoid entering the village as the streets are narrow so try the unpaved car park area just before the crossroads. Use the church spire as a landmark and take a wander around the village.

Coll de Rates **N38°43.431 W0°03.571**

Use the car park if you are stopping for the restaurant or use any of the viewpoints along the mountain pass, these are ideal for picnics.

Polop Village Centre **N38°37.386 W0°07.941**

The streets in the village are narrow, so it is best to park on the waste ground, then cross the roundabout and walk into the village centre.

Day Out Javea

Javea, known as Xábia in Valencian, is a pretty holiday resort town with more than enough to keep everyone entertained for a great day out! It is situated in a wide bay between the rocky headlands of the Cap of San Antoni and the Cap La Nao. Each headland has a lighthouse, a selection of walking paths and absolutely stunning views. There are three distinct beach areas, all of which have their own characteristics and a great marina with a selection of top class fish restaurants.

The historic centre is situated a few kilometres inland as its original inhabitants feared attacks from marauding pirates. The narrow streets with their wrought iron balconies, large wooden front doors and stone porticoes make it a great place for an amble.

Javea Viewpoint Cap de San Antoni **N38°48.228 E0°11.570**

Parking is in the gravelled car park and is free, there are a number of marked walking trails, information boards and right at the end of the road is the fenced off lighthouse.

Javea Marina **N38°47.859 E0°11.045**

Parking is on the side of the road or in the marina and is free.

Javea Beach North End **N38°47.434 E0°10.898**

Parking at Platja de Benissero is free and is on the actual shingle beach.

Javea Old Town **N38°47.371 E0°09.652**

Parking is in the underground pay car at the Plaza de la Constitucion, exit the car park and follow the signs to the historic quarter.

Javea Beach Central **N38°46.261 E0°11.494**

Parking at Platja de L'Arenal is in the car park or in any of the marked parking spaces on either side of the road and is free.

Javea Beach South End **N38°45.795 E0°12.282**

Parking for Cala Blanca is in the small car park which is a dead end, or in any of the spaces before the car park and is free.

Javea Viewpoint Cap de la Nau **N38°43.981 E0°13.719**

Parking is in the car park and is free, there are a number of marked walking paths, viewpoints with information boards, a fenced off lighthouse and two restaurants with amazing panoramic terraces!

Day Out La Manga Strip

The La Manga Strip is a piece of land that separates the Mediterranean Sea from the Mar Menor. La Manga is Spanish for sleeve and aptly describes this 21 kilometre long, 300 metre wide spit. A day out to the La Manga Strip can be enjoyed during summer when it is very busy or during winter when it is quiet, with most establishments being closed.

The strip encloses the Mar Menor which directly translates as the small sea, although it is the largest lagoon in Europe. It has a surface area of 130 square kilometres and a maximum depth of 8 metres. The crystal clear waters are warm, calm and rich in salts and minerals, in fact the temperature never falls below 18 degrees.

All along the Strip on both sides, there are beautiful beaches with white sands, rocky outcrops, marinas and plenty of water sport schools. A great selection of bars, cafes, restaurants, hotels and tourist shops amongst other facilities line the road.

Punta Brava **N37°41.376 W0°50.443**

Parking on the road and either follow the marked walking route around the hill and enjoy the views from the top, or for the less energetic park further up the road and admire the views from there.

La Manga High Street **N37°39.318 W0°43.251**

This is the start of the Strip. There are many 'commercial zones' on both sides, so explore at your leisure, as there is only one road along the Strip you really can't get lost!!

La Manga Beaches **N37°39.318 W0°43.251**

This is just one of the 15 or so beaches along the length of the Strip, so stop anywhere you see a sign for 'playa'. The sea is a lot warmer on the Mar Menor side than the Mediterranean side of the Strip!

La Manga Marina Tomas Maestre **N37°44.571 W0°44.487**

Parking is in the marina and is free. There are two 'parades' of places to eat and drink. When at the roundabout just after the entrance arches turn right for modern parade with views of the marina, or turn left for a more ramshackle parade with views to the Mar Menor.

Boat Trip La Manga to Santiago de la Ribera

The B&F ferries depart all year round from the little jetty beside the club house (at the roundabout just after the entrance arches turn right and continue to the very end) across to Santiago de la Ribera on the other side of the Mar Menor. There is normally a notice board with the current timetable beside the jetty with a round trip taking about 2 hours.

🔗For the most up to date information, timetables and prices take a look at the official link on the website.

Day Out Mar Menor

The Mar Menor, meaning little sea, is a unique sea lagoon and well worth a visit. It is separated from the Mediterranean by a narrow piece of land called the La Manga Strip, which protrudes from Cabo de Palos at the south end of the Mar Menor and continues for 21 kilometres towards San Pedro at the north end, where it creates a small channel to allow water in and out of the Mar Menor. The waters enclosed by the strip are always calm, never colder than 18oC and are very rich in salts and iodine making it unique.

There are lots of little villages dotted around the shores of the Mar Menor. We have put together a full day out with three stops as a taster, but you might like to spend the whole day in each place or just visit two of them! Los Alcazares is a charming seaside town with long promenade to stroll along. Punta Brava is a small village with a fantastic viewpoint from where you'll get amazing vistas across the Mar Menor, the Strip and the Sierra Mineras. Cabo de Palos has a quaint marina and a rocky coastline to explore. From here you can drive along the La Manga Strip, but be aware that it is not linked to the mainland at the end, so you have to drive the full 21 kilometres back again!

Los Alcazares **N37°44.165 W0°51.072**

Parking is in a car park and is free. The beach, marina and promenade are in front of you, just turn left as the beach to the right is fenced off for military use. Take a stop at the Hotel Balneario La Encarnacion, a former spa hotel which has a magnificent internal courtyard, go inside, past the bar and into the patio.

Punta Brava **N37°41.376 W0°50.443**

Parking is on the road, either follow the marked walking route around the hill and enjoy the views from the top, or for the less energetic park further up the road and admire the views from here

Cabo de Palos **N37°37.989 W0°42.100**

Parking is in a car park and is free. The marina is in front of you. The sandy beach is accessed via the streets on the opposite side of the marina to where the boats are moored, and the rocky headland is to the right of the beach and at the mouth of the marina.

Cabo de Palos Lighthouse **N37°38.020 W0°41.466**

Parking is in the car park and is free, alternatively you can park near the marina and walk!

Day Out Mar Menor Mud Baths

The town of San Pedro del Pinatar and the suburb of Lo Pagan are situated on the north shore of the Mar Menor and are a great destination for a day out.

The Salinas de San Pedro Regional Park has a really informative visitors centre where you can learn all about the sand dunes and salt marshes as well as the fauna and flora of the park. Then take a drive through the park, stopping to explore the paths and enjoy a coffee at the marina overlooking the boats.

The mud baths in the Lo Pagan area of the town are free to use, which is great news if you have a large family to keep occupied. Everyone can try the mud baths, but only the truly hardy indulge during the winter months. Simply walk down the steps, cover yourself with the therapeutic mud, said to be good for all types of skin complaints, aches and pain, dry off in the sun, then re-enter the water to wash it all off!

For the energetic, the salt marshes and mud baths form a fantastic circular 12 kilometre cycling or walking route.

San Pedro Visitors Centre **N37°50.071 W0°46.713**

Visit the centre for information about the regional park and to see its various exhibits and collect a map and leaflet. Entrance is free and it is open all year.

🔗For the most up to date information about opening times and prices take a look at the official link on the website.

San Pedro Marina and Beach **N37°49.195 W0°45.469**

For the older area of the marina walk through the arch with the sign Plaza Ocio and for the newer area and the beach continue along the road to the next car park.

San Pedro Salt Marshes **N37°49.398 W0°45.630**

Parking is in any of the car parking areas that you pass on the road going to the marina, follow any of the walking and cycling paths running through this regional park.

Lo Pagan Mud Baths **N37°49.236 W0°46.581**

Park for free in any of the spaces alongside the road then, starting from the windmill go along the elevated walking and cycling route. Walk down the wooden steps into the mud baths, collect some of the therapeutic mud, rub it onto your skin, let it dry and then go back down the wooden steps to wash it! The mud baths are free to use and are open all year.

Walking & Cycling Route **N37°50.071 W0°46.713**

Starting this 12 kilometre route from the Visitor Centre, take the path alongside the road to Lo Pagan, turn left at the windmill and go along the elevated salinas walking and cycling route out to sea, follow it around to the left, you'll feel like you can almost touch the hotels on the La Manga Strip. Either head straight for the beach, or follow any of the trails through the sand dunes, there are no right or wrong routes and the terrain changes between hard ground, dried mud and sand so you need to be a bit adventurous! Continue past the marina and the salt marshes before arriving back at the visitors centre.

Day Out Mazarron Area

Mazarron is situated in the Costa Calida which is the name for the coastal area of the province of Murcia, all 250km of it! Costa Calida means the warm coast, and is so called because of the hot mean annual temperatures and the limited rainfall of only 34cm per year!

This route is all about getting to know the area and its towns, ports, coastline and mountains. We have put together a full day out with six stops as a taster, but you might like to spend longer in each place.

It starts with a journey along the toll road, guaranteed to be quiet as most locals like to avoid paying them. The first stop is at the historic old town of Mazarron for a bit of exploring and a coffee. Afterwards it is a short drive to the coast to see the amazingly weird sand sculptures of Bolnuevo. The view point, above the beach, gives you a clear idea of the rockiness of the Costa Calidas coastline. Then it is onto the Port of Mazarron, for a stroll beside the marina. A stop at Isla Plana for the short promenade, church and quaint harbour. More scenery as you leave and enter the mountain pass in the direction of Cartagena, pausing at the viewpoint before heading home.

You can easily add a stop at the marina in the coastal city of Cartagena or, as you start the mountain pass slip off to the Cartagena Guns at Cabo Tinoso, the choice is yours!

Mazarron Inland Town **N37°35.654 W1°19.078**

Parking is on the road and is free. The centre is a short walk away, go towards the roundabout with the statue of a miner and a fountain on it, turn left and walk uphill to the town square for the Town Hall (they will give you a map), bars and cafes, Veles Castle, San Andres Church, La Purisma Church and the Saturday morning market.

Bolnuevo **N37°33.802 W1°18.715**

Parking is in the car park and is free, the sand sculptures are on one side and the beautiful long fine sandy beach is on the other side! Explore and enjoy.

Bolnuevo Viewpoint **N37°33.810 W1°18.995**

This a 'photo and go' stop with stunning views along the rugged cliffs of the Costa Calida, over the sand sculptures and back towards Mazarron inland town.

Mazarron Coastal Town & Marina **N37°33.880 W1°15.508**

Parking is in the underground car park and is charged for by the length of stay, exit the car park and walk along past the boats of the marina for the cafes and bars.

Isla Plana **N37°34.476 W1°12.528**

Parking is on the road and is free, walk along the short promenade to see the Roman remains and church, or follow the pavement towards Mazarron to discover the quaint harbour.

Sierra de la Muela Viewpoint **N37°35.136 W1°09.406**

This is another 'photo and go' stop with stunning views back to places you have visited today!

Day Out Mula, Bullas and Cehegin

The inland part of the province of Murcia is just as delightful and worth visiting as the coastal part. It has spectacular scenery as it lies within the Espuna and Revolcadores Mountains along the course of the Mula river. There are many charming towns and villages which have been inhabited since prehistoric times and plenty of unique culture as this area has been relatively isolated throughout history.

This day out is designed to give you a good feel for the area, but there is so much to see and do in all three places that you might prefer to spend the whole day visiting only one of them. Or perhaps you can 'mix and match' these destinations with Caravaca, Moratalla or Calasparra that make up the other day out to inland Murcia.

Mula is a great place for a morning coffee and an explore. Bullas has an interesting wine museum and many, many bodegas to visit. Cehegin is quite simply a delight, a walk through its narrow streets up to the town hall is a must.

The Via Verde is a cycling and walking path running along the route of the old Murcia - Caravaca railway which closed in 1971. The route is 48km from Caravaca, past Cehegin, Bullas and Mula.

Mula **N38°02.419 W1°29.593**

Parking is in the street and is free, expect on Saturdays as it is closed for the weekly market. Walk along this main street for the town hall square, known as the Plaza del Ayuntamiento, then explore the town, you can even follow the signs up to the castle ruins.

Bullas Wine Museum **N38°03.050 W1°39.900**

Parking is in the street and is free. The museum is located in an old wine cellar that used to produce 350,000 litres of wine annually. The exhibits display everything about the wine industry including past and present techniques.

🔗 For the most up to date information about opening times and prices take a look at the official link on the website.

Bullas **N38°03.011 W1°40.115**

Parking is on the street and is free, do not drive into the old town as the streets are extremely narrow. Walk back to the main road, turn right for the old town or go straight ahead for the new town.

Cehegin **N38°05.524 W1°47.925**

Parking is in the car park and is free, alternatively you can park in any of the streets. From here cross the roundabout with the water fountain on it and enter the old town via the steps.

Day Out Ricote Valley

The whole day is all about scenery, history and relaxation. Starting at the northerly end of the valley in Cieza, which was a major settlement during Moorish time and today is an agricultural town producing mainly peaches and olives. The next stop, is a short drive away at Abaran to see the Noria Grande or the Big Waterwheel. Take a stroll along the River Segura to discover more waterwheels, all of which transport water from the river to irrigate the most distant plains. Driving on through the valley you can take a deviation up to the village of Ricote, which is a delightful little hamlet with a few restaurants and lots of Moorish architecture. Returning to the valley floor, enjoy the views as you make your way slowly via Ojos and Villanueva to the Balneario in Archena with its thermal pools.

You can alter the day in many ways. You might like to add a stop at the small hamlets of Ojos and Villanueva as you pass through them on driving along the base of the valley, or spend the whole day in Cieza, or in Abaran walking or cycling along the Rio Segura between the waterwheels or at the thermal baths in Archena. You can even fit in a stop at the shopping malls on the outskirts of Murcia as you drive past them - remember they are open until 22.00!

Cieza **N38°14.077 W1°24.853**

Parking is on the road near the school (colegio) and is free. There are a few cafes nearby, ideal for a coffee and cake. To explore the town walk back along the road that you have just driven along to the roundabout with the Arabic looking stone arches on it and turn left, walk straight on to the top of this street for the tourist office.

Abaran **N38°12.387 W1°24.128**

Parking is on the road near the school (colegio) and is free. Walk down the slope opposite the school to see the waterwheel and continue through the park to find the river. For a short walk along the river turn right when facing the river, for a longer walk along the route of the four waterwheels turn left and continue beside the river.

Ricote **N38°09.127 W1°21.928**

Parking is on the road and is free. Spend some time exploring the streets of this pretty small village and admire the views and fresh air, a good chance to stretch your legs, head to the church to discover the heart of the village.

Archena Spa **N38°07.762 W1°18.429**

Parking is in the multi story resort car park. The Archena Thermal Baths has 2 large and modern thermal pools where the water is maintained at 34-36oC. There are also saunas of different temperatures and humidity, massage rooms, crosscurrent pools, warm hammocks, salt water floatation pools and much more. The thermal baths are open to non-hotel guests (you must take a swim hat, flip-flops and towels).

🔗For the most up to date information about opening times and prices take a look at the official link on the website.

Day Out Scenic Train Journey Los Nietos to Cartagena

This great day out starts with a stop in the small village of Los Nietos on the shores of the Mar Menor. After enjoying a morning coffee at any of the beach front cafes, and exploring the village with it's beach and marina, make your way to the train station.

Trains run every half an hour from 07:00 in the morning to 20:00 in the evening from Monday to Saturday, so you'll never have to wait long. You can always check out the timetables beforehand. There are 15 stops on this journey along the feve operated narrow gauge line, most of which are at tiny hamlets. However the train does stop at the larger town of La Union which hosts a lively market every Tuesday morning in the streets near to the train station.

The scenery along the route is stunning, as the line passes through the Sierra Mineras. These are a rolling mountain range that has been mined since Roman times, so there is plenty to enjoy along the way.

After half an hour the train terminates in the sub train station (three minutes walk to the main train station) in the city of Cartagena. The main train station is easily recognisable by the 'lighthouse clock tower' that sits on top of it! Across the road is the tourist office, so pop in to collect a map before exploring the narrow streets of the old town, or selecting a place for an enjoyable 'Menu del Dia'. Alternatively walk beside the old city wall towards the marina and then follow our Cartagena City walking route on page 74. Then it is back on the train to Los Nietos and your car.

Los Nietos Village **N37°39.018 W0°47.332**

Parking is on the road and is free, then wander down onto the beach for the promenade and the marina.

Los Nietos Train Station **N37°39.108 W0°47.835**

Parking is in the designated car park area and is free. There is only one platform as this is the end of the line. The train runs roughly every 30 minutes the journey to Cartagena takes about half an hour.

🔗For the most up to date information, timetables and prices take a look at the official link on the website.

Cartagena City **N37°36.217 W0°58.612**

You'll be arriving by train into the sub train station which is situated beside the main station that looks like a lighthouse clock tower. Then cross the road to the tourist office and collect a map.

Day Out Sierra Mineras

This day is packed with stunning scenery, so make sure that you choose any one of the 300 or so bright, sunshiny, blue sky days that the province of Murcia has. You can easily spend a whole day leisurely driving along this route, stopping where and when you want or combine it with a morning in the City of Cartagena or the afternoon in any of the towns and villages around the Mar Menor such as Cabo de Palos, Punta Brava or Los Alcazares.

Once you have passed Cartagena the first stop along this route is at the small cove of Cala Cortina, the nearest beach to the city. Then following the signs for Escombreras continue through the somewhat surreal industrial port with all of its heavy machinery, warehouses and the Repsol oil refinery. After this you enter the Sierra Mineras. These have been mined since pre-historic times right up to the mid 20th century. The mine shafts, wheels, tunnels, trains, tracks and equipment have simply been abandoned. This, coupled with the beautiful colours of the exposed minerals makes for an interesting drive. You can pull off into the small marina and beach at Portman and call into the famous and pricey La Manga Golf Resort before heading home.

Cala Cortina **N37°34.918 W0°58.477**

Parking is in the car park and is free, walk down the steps to the small sandy cove with it's picturesque views and restaurant.

Escombreras **N37°34.407 W0°54.563**

This isn't a stop, but a way marker to keep you on the right road past all of the industrial units including a huge Iberdrola power plant and Repsol refinery.

Portman Marina & Playa Lastre **N37°34.817 W0°50.512**

Parking is in the car park beside the tiny marina and is free. Walk along the short promenade to the black sandy beach or climb the cliff to the lighthouse.

La Manga Golf Resort **N37°36.214 W0°48.158**

Parking is in the car park areas and is free. This is the location on the prestigious La Manga Golf Resort, but there are over 20 other bars and restaurants to try dotted around the 3 championship golf courses.

Day Out Villajoyosa and Cuevas del Canelobre

Villajoyosa as it is known in Spanish or La Vila Joiosa as it is called by the local people in Valencian literally means the 'joyful village'. It is famous as a centre for the production of chocolate, which could be the reason for its name! The town has three chocolate factories, all of which can be visited. The Valor Chocolate factory is perhaps the most famous, but there is also the Perez Factory and the Clavileno Factory, so you'll be spoilt for choice! Villajoyosa has over 3 kilometres of beaches, a lovely marina, a beach front promenade and the iconic multi coloured houses of the fisherman.

The magnificent Caves of Canelobre are said to be Spain's largest and deepest cave system. It is open all year, doesn't close for siesta and can only be visited as part of a guided tour – take warm clothes as it is cold inside! The views from the entrance are simply stunning, and there is a small picnic area so you can admire the vistas whilst enjoying your sandwiches and waiting for the next tour to begin.

The caves were formed many millions of years ago, but they are still slowly changing at a rate of just 1cm every 100 years! The stalactites and stalagmites are continuously growing and aided by the clever lighting take on the shapes and forms of all sorts of animals as well as giving the caves a cathedral like feel. The main attraction is the candelabra formation, from which the caves have taken their name.

Villajoyosa Car Park **N38°30.307 W0°13.800**

Parking is in the underground car park and is charged for by length of stay. Take a walk along the sandy beach and promenade which are backed by the icon multi coloured houses of the fisherman.

Villajoyosa Valor Chocolate Factory **N38°30.722 W0°13.975**

Parking is on the side of the road around the Valor Factory. The free tours generally run every half hour, if you want to be sure of a specific time then call in advance and reserve your place.

🔗 For the most up to date information about opening times take a look at the official link on the website.

Cuevas del Canelobre Car Park **N38°30.670 W0°24.720**

Parking is in the free car park beside the entrance to the caves, souvenir shop, toilets and picnic area.

🔗For the most up to date information about opening times and prices take a look at the official link on the website.

Day Out Yecla and Vineyards

This day out starts with a coffee stop in the unusual but sweet village of La Romana. It is unusual because the actual layout of the village was planned to be like a grid, so it makes it very easy to explore. It is worth stretching you legs and wandering around the grand village square and the nearby church.

Driving through the 'huerto' the Spanish name given to cultivated countryside, passing Monover and Pinoso you'll see lots of little bodegas, so stop and sample as you wish!! On the outskirts of Yecla is the largest producer of the area called the La Purisina Co-operative bodega. Take time to visit the small shop and try the excellent value locally produced wine (closed during siesta).

Yecla makes a perfect lunch stop for a picnic or restaurant. It has several places of interest including the Sanctuary Virgin del Castillo. It is lovely to wander up the steep roads, past the impressive churches to soak up the atmosphere of this characterful inland town.

We suggest completing the circular route by returning via the motorway, past the furniture stores, the production of which is the other main industry within the area. Then through the Vinalope Valley along the motorway known as the route of the castles.

Albatera **N38°11.088 W0°52.327**

This isn't an actual stop, but a drive through so that you approach the Sierras de Crevillent along the correct road - the CV873.

Hondon de las Nieves **N38°18.526 W0°51.285**

This isn't an actual stop, but you can park and explore if you wish. We advise visiting Hondon de las Nieves as part of Day Out Hondon and Novelda.

La Romana **N38°21.930 W0°53.770**

Parking is on the road and is free. A great place for your morning coffee, walk into the streets on your left to explore the village centre.

Yecla La Purisina Bodega **N38°36.544 W1°06.151**

Parking is on the road, right beside the shop for this vineyard, so pop in and try and buy some of the locally produced wine.

🔗For the most up to date information about the bodega take a look at the official link on the website.

Yecla **N38°36.544 W1°06.151**

Parking is on the road and is free, you can park closer to the town centre, but the streets are very narrow and parking spaces extremely limited. Walk back to the main road, cross over and turn right and walk towards the Parque de la Constitucion. Continue up the main high street Calle San Francisco to the Plaza Espana, where the tourist office is located. Stop and explore where you like!

Half Day Out Scenic Drive Pedrera Reservoir

The scenic drive around the reservoir twinned with a stop for a coffee at the start, a walk around the village of Torremendo and a meal at the hamlet of Rebate or the Castle in San Miguel makes for a great morning or afternoon out.

The man made reservoir known as the Embalse de la Pedrera is always a delight to drive around. It offers a constantly changing vista depending on the weather conditions, time of day and how full of water it is. You can pack a picnic and find a place to sit and admire the views over the reservoir, which has been dammed to provide a constant source of water for the area. Although there are no official cycling paths, if you are feeling fit you can easily cycle all the way around on the road!

Torremendo is a small village situated close to the shores of the Embalse de la Pedrera reservoir. It consists of only a few streets centred around the traditional church square. The neighbouring hamlet of Rebate is even smaller and has a tiny chapel within the grounds of the Rebate restaurant. The Castle of Condesa stands at the very end of the route, a recently refurbished Moorish castle it is now a restaurant.

Start of Driving Route **N38°01.483 W0°50.170**

This isn't an actual stop, but a marker so that you approach the reservoir along the correct road.

Embalse de la Pedrera Dam **N38°01.969 W0°52.546**

This is another marker to help you stay on the correct road. There are no official viewpoints but you can stop wherever it is safe to do so and admire the view or have a picnic. Be extremely careful if you are going to leave your car and walk down onto the shores of the reservoir, it is well known that petty thieves operate here.

Torremendo **N37°59.514 W0°51.925**

Parking is on the road, take a wander around this small village.

Rebate **N37°56.493 W0°52.131**

Parking is in the car park and is free. There is a little chapel close by this popular restaurant as well as a duck pond full of ducks and peacocks!

End of Driving Route **N37°58.294 W0°47.574**

This is the third way marker, so that you finish your drive along a scenic road, passing by the restored Moorish Castle the Castillo de Conesa which has a restaurants and children's play area.

Day Out Sierra Espuna Regional Park

The Regional Park of Sierra Espuna is absolutely stunning! It is located inland in the province of Murcia and covers some 25,000 hectares. It has been protected since 1930 and in 1992 it was classified as a Regional Park. Pine trees cover most of the park and, as it has some 20 mountain peaks above 1,000 meters the views over the top of the pine forests are magnificent. It takes its name from its highest mountain, the Espuna at 1583 meters!

The park has quite an intriguing history. The region of Murica enjoyed great prosperity during the 18th century when it plundered its natural resources including its pine forests. When Ricardo Codorniu, a passionate nature lover and forest engineer returned to the region in 1889, he was devastated by the destruction caused by the years of economic boom. He set about restoring the forest, replanting 19,000 hectares and became known as the 'apostle of tress'. As you drive though the park you'll notice evidence of his hard work as a lot of the pine trees are planted in straight lines.

Today the park is criss crossed with many kilometres of marked walking and cycling routes. The mountain road is well maintained and there are numerous panoramic viewpoints as well as some great picnic and barbecue areas. You might even see the wild boars, mountain goats and circling eagles during your scenic drive.

Sanctuary of Santa Eulalia **N37°47.931 W1°33.498**

Parking is in the car park and is free. Explore the gardens and enjoy a morning coffee in the restaurant and take a look inside the church which has been beautifully decorated in the Mudejar style.

Viewpoint del Cristo **N37°47.863 W1°33.196**

Parking is on the gravelled area and is free. On a clear day you'll see the sea at Mazarron in one direction and the mountains of the Sierra Nevadas in the other!

Aledo **N37°47.746 W1°34.403**

Parking is in the marked parking area and is free. Walk through the quiet streets of the village towards the tower del Homenaje. It was built in the 11th century to control the valley below. Go in and climb the steps to the top for more amazing views! Inside the tower is a tourist office and exhibitions about the tower and the village. It is free to visit and is open every morning all year.

Ice Storage Huts **N37°52.170 W1°34.068**

This is a small detour and the road is only open from 08:00-18:00! From the car parking area it is a 5 minute walk to the ice storage huts. One has been renovated whilst the other two are in a ruined state. They were used from the 16th century right up until the 1920's to store the winter snow well into the hot summers.

Picnic & Barbecue Area del Hilo **N37°51.485 W1°31.377**

Parking is in the car park area and is free. There are barbecues which you can use during the winter; bring your own charcoal, fire-lighters, matches, meat and enjoy! Alternatively there is a restaurant that leaves out food for the wild bores, so if you're lucky they might be enjoying their lunch too!! The Forest House is a short walk away it is a handsomely restored building which contains an exhibition geared toward children about the park's history and the wildlife.

Visitors Centre **N37°51.340 W1°30.727**

Parking is in the car park and is free. The Visitors Centre has permanent exhibition about the flora and fauna of the park as well as some information on walking routes.

Alhama de Murcia **N37°51.108 W1°25.656**

Parking is beside the road and is free. Explore the Plaza Americas in front of you then follow the signs to the Centro Viejo for the old town with its multi coloured houses. There is a Roman Baths Museum as well as the impressive 11th century Castillo de Alhama which sits high on the hill above Alhama de Murcia.

Days Out in Alicante City

Alicante is a city which has it all; a vibrant historic section with the Castle of Santa Barbara as it's crowning glory, a traditional bull ring, long fine sandy beaches, an impressive marina from where you can take the boat to the Island of Tabarca or across the marina to the Panorama Centre, a great selection of boutiques, department stores and specialist shops, and many fiestas including the famous Hogueras or Bonfires around the end of June.

Santa Barbara Castle is well worth a visit. If you are feeling energetic, you can walk the 166m to the top through the old quarter, take the tourist bus or catch the lift from the street. However, the best way is to drive and park for free! You can explore the well preserved castle ruins at your own pace, taking in the stunning views and the tranquillity of its setting. On a clear day you'll look out over the marina and beaches to the sea, down onto the cathedral and the old town, you'll see the bullring and the football stadium for Hercules Alicante as well as the mountains in the distance.

Visit the Tourist Office for information about the museums and other places of interest. Remember that most museums are closed on a Monday and for siesta which is generally 14.00-16.00 in the winter and 14.00-17.00 in the summer.

Itinerary 1

To get to know the city in one day, park at the marina and follow our walking route around the city. You'll discover the tourist office, the old quarter known as the barrio, the free Nativity and Hogueres Museums, and if you want to make a small deviation you can visit the bull ring and it's museum, which is also free. Enjoy a menu del dia for lunch, then drive up to the Santa Barbara Castle where it is free to park and visit. Or take a picnic with you to eat at the castle and relax in the peace and tranquillity, whilst enjoying the views out over the Mediterranean and inland towards the mountains.

Alicante Marina Car Park **N38°20.451 W0°28.716**

Parking is in the underground car park beside the Marina and is charged for by length of stay.

The Nativity Museum or Museo de Belenes is free to visit and includes many nativity scenes and individual figurines.

🔗For the latest information check the official link on the website.

The Hogueras Museum or Museo de Fogueres is free and contains a large collection of ninots, the beautifully sculptured statues which are burnt during the San Juan Fiesta during June.

For the latest information check the official link on the website.

The Bull Ring or Plaza de Tores and its Museum are free to visit, although the bull ring is only open during the mornings.

For the latest information check the official link on the website.

St Barbara Castle **N38°20.943 W0°28.602**

Parking is in the free castle car park or you can use the city centre car park and either walk up, take the tourist bus or use the lift. It is free to explore the Castillo de Santa Barbara, which has a cafe, toilets and picnic tables with stunning views out over the sea. The castle is open: all day, every day and is great when everything else closes for siesta.

For the latest information check the official link on the website.

Itinerary 2

Park at the marina and walk along the promenade beside the Postiguet beach for a relaxing coffee at any of the beach front cafes. Retrace your steps and amble beside the marina, enjoying the boats from dry land. If it is a weekend or fiesta take the little shuttle boat across the marina to the other side. Next, head into the shopping district for the El Corte Ingles Department store and other high street names. Have a leisurely lunch and walk back down to the sea, stopping before the marina on the Explanada de Espana, with its iconic wavy patterned tiles and permanent market stalls. As you leave the city, stop at the El Palmeral Park for a wander around its trails below the majestic palm trees.

Alicante Marina Car Park **N38°20.451 W0°28.716**

Parking is in the underground car park beside the Marina and is charged for by length of stay.

Alicante City Palmeral Park **N38°19.224 W0°30.824**

Parking is in the car park beside the park and is free.

Playa del Postiguet Beach with over half a kilometre of fine golden sand, it is located right in the heart of the city.

Marina Shuttle operates at weekends and fiestas only and leaves from the mooring beside the statue of the man with a surf board or Icarus with one of his wings, no one is quite sure which!

El Palmeral Park has paths, streams, waterfalls, a boating lake, bmx track and many, many palm tress. It is open everyday in winter 09:00-23:00 and in summer 09:00-24:00.

Itinerary 3

Park at the marina and walk up to the castle through the old neighbourhood known as the Santa Cruz district, arriving at the castle for a refreshing drink. Then purchase a day ticket for the tourist bus and hop on and off it as often as you please whilst discovering the city, or return via the escalator. Finish the day relaxing at any of the cafes along the beach or in the marina.

Alicante Marina Car Park **N38°20.451 W0°28.716**

Parking is in the underground car park beside the Marina and is charged for by length of stay.

St Barbara Castle Car Park **N38°20.943 W0°28.602**

This can be visited by walking up and down to it, using the lift, taking the tourist bus or driving and parking at the castle.

For the lift: exit the marina car park, walk towards the beach and cross the main road, continue along Av. Juan Bautista Lafora to the entrance.

For the latest information check the official link on the website.

The walk: takes about 35-40 mins each way not allowing for any stops to admire the view, take pictures or have a little rest! There is no right or wrong route, on the way up simply follow the signs to the Parque de la Ereta and on the way down, head for the marina.

Route Up: exit the marina car park, follow the walking route through the Plaza del Ayuntamiento and past the Nativity Museum, from there head straight on and you'll see the signs for the park, once inside the park head for the restaurant and you'll find the path to take you to the castle entrance on the inland side of Mount Benacantil, the last section of which is along the road.

Route Down: leave the castle along the road on the inland side of Mount Benacantil and follow this to the first bend, from here you'll see signs to the park, follow any of these routes and keep heading downhill with the marina in front of you.

Alicante City Tourist Bus

Exit the marina car park, cross the road towards the beach and at the big roundabout is the Turi Bus Stop. This is a hop on hop off service with audio commentary available in 6 languages explaining all the interesting points along the journey. Tickets are valid for the whole day and for all of the 10 stops, including the Santa Barbara Castle.

🔗For the latest information check the official link on the website.

Alicante Football Hércules CF

Hércules Club de Fútbol was founded in 1922, and generally plays in the Spanish La Liga or Second Division A. It has a 30,000 seater stadium called the Estadio José Rico Pérez.

🔗For the latest information, fixture list and ticket prices check the official link on the website.

Alicante Football Stadium **N38°21.591 W0°29.754**

Visit by train

To avoid driving and parking in the city, you can visit Alicante by train from Orihuela or San Isidro (Albatera-Catral). The train station is opposite the El Corte Ingles department store, right on the edge of the main shopping area, so walk and explore. The marina is about a 15 minute walk away, or you can join our city walking route at the Hogueras Museum, which is about 7 minutes away on foot.

Alicante City Walking Map

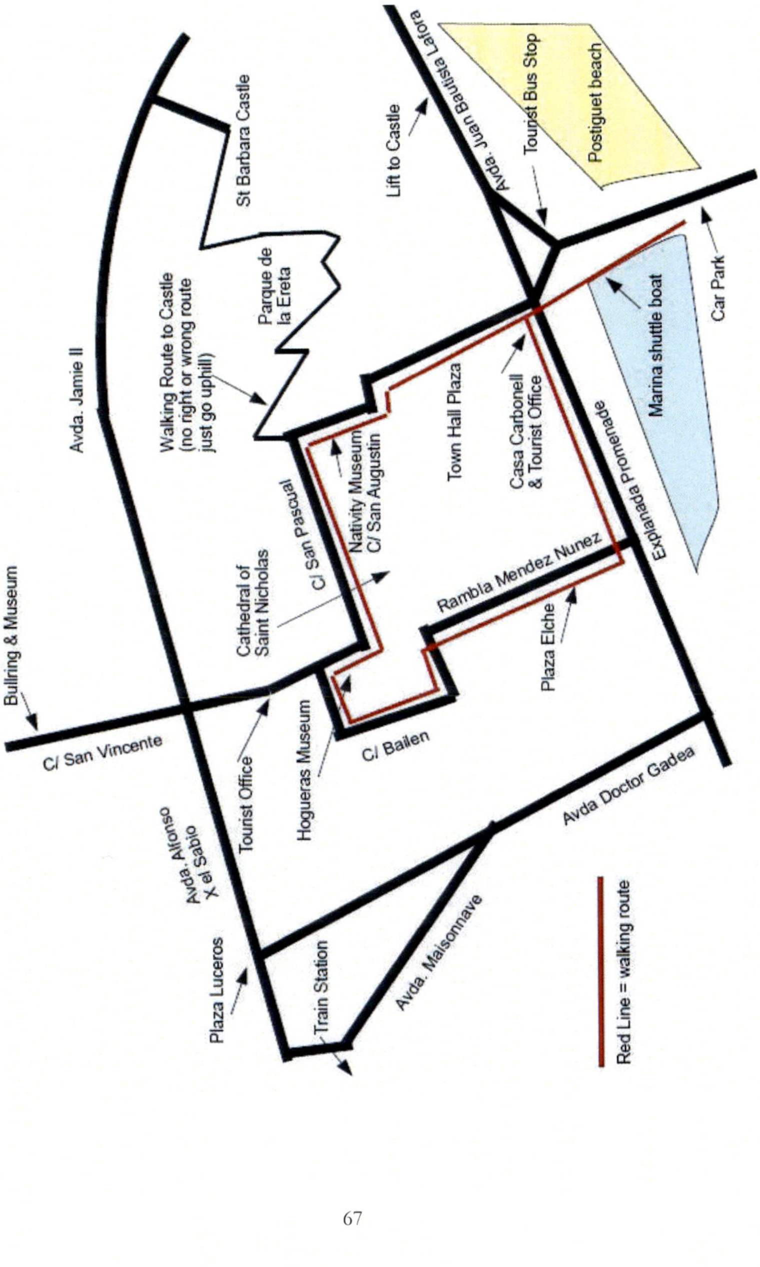

Days Out in Cartagena City

Cartagena is a charming, compact, coastal city that became great during the Roman times when Hannibal set off from it with his elephants on his journey to Rome. There are so many things to see, with over 12 museums, 10 buildings of interest, 4 noteworthy churches and a whole host of monuments not to mention the archaeological sites. You can take the very informative Tourist Bus or perhaps sail out to sea on the Tourist Boat. You can explore the narrow characterful streets of the old town or relax at one of the bars, cafes and restaurants on the waterfront. A cruise ship may even be visiting, as Cartagena's port is the third deepest in the world.

Visit the Tourist Office for information about the museums and other places of interest. Remember that most museums are closed on a Monday and for siesta which is generally 14.00-16.00 in the winter and 14.00-17.00 in the summer.

Itinerary 1

To get to know the city in one day, park at the marina and start your day with a trip on the tourist boat to receive a good introduction to this fascinating city. After a spot of lunch follow our walking route around the city. You'll discover the main tourist office, the entrance to the Roman Theatre Museum and the impressive buildings of the casino, the Grand Hotel, the Arsenal and the Captains Residence.

Cartagena Marina Car Park **N37°35.876 W0°59.052**

Parking is in the underground car park beside the marina and is charged for by length of stay.

Cartagena City Tourist Boat

Exit the marina car park and walk along the promenade to the tourist boat mooring in front of the restaurants. It is a 60 minute journey around the harbour with narrative about the area.

For the most up to date information, timetables and prices take a look at the official link on the website.

Itinerary 2

Cartagena has more than 12 museums for you to explore so spend the morning visiting some of them. The Roman Theatre which was only discovered in 1987 is a firm favourite, but there are many others to try!

For the afternoon drive the short distance to Cartagenas only beach, Cala Cortina where there is a restaurant or bring your own picnic. The journey takes you past the industrial harbour, stopping at the viewpoint for a great photo back towards the city.

Cartagena Marina Car Park **N37°35.876 W0°59.052**

Parking is in the underground car park beside the marina and is charged for by length of stay.

Cartagena City Roman Theatre

Marked on the city walking route, there are two parts to the Roman Theatre Museum; the actual theatre and an exhibition room.

For the most up to date information about opening times and prices take a look at the official link on the website.

Cartagena City Cala Cortina **N37°34.918 W0°58.477**

This is the closest beach to the city and makes a lovely stop at the start or end of a day in Cartagena There are some great view points along the way and a picturesque restaurant once you arrive.

Itinerary 3

Park at the marina and start your day with a trip around the city on the Tourist Bus. The narrative on the bus will tell you all about Cartagenas fascinating history, and introduce you to most of its many museums. Afterwards walk to the top of Conception hill or, for a more sedate option take the panoramic lift and have a tour around the Castle of Conception for a complete history on Cartagena and some great views of the city. Then treat yourself to a late lunch when the shops and museums close for siesta or visit the ARQUA, the National Museum of Underwater Archaeology which remains open all day.

Cartagena Marina Car Park **N37°35.876 W0°59.052**

Parking is in the underground car park beside the marina and is charged for by length of stay.

Cartagena City Tourist Bus

The tourist bus stop is behind the restaurants on the promenade beside the marina. This is a 45 minute journey taking in the main places of interest with an audio guide in several languages, so you can decide where to visit afterwards.

🔗For the most up to date information, timetables and prices take a look at the official link on the website.

Cartagena City Castle of Conception

The Castle of Conception, or Castillo de la Concepcion, in Spanish, is located on Cerro de la Concepcion, one of five hills that protect the city. The centre was built in the remains of the castle and is an interactive exhibition about the history of the city.

🔗For the most up to date information about opening times and prices take a look at the official link on the website.

Panoramic Lift

Use the glass lift to access the Castle of Concepcion and to enjoy some stunning views of the city. It is a great alternative to walking up!

🔗For the most up to date information, timetables and prices take a look at the official link on the website.

ARQUA National Museum of Underwater Archaeology

Lots of interactive exhibits about the rich underwater cultural heritage of Spain and its conservation.

🔗For the most up to date information about opening times and prices take a look at the official link on the website.

Cartagena Football Club

Fútbol Club Cartagena is based in Cartagena. It was founded in 1995 and usually plays in the Spanish Second Division A or B. It has a 15,105 seater stadium, called the Estadio Cartagonova.

🔗For the latest information, fixture list and ticket prices check the official link on the website.

Cartagena Football Stadium **N37°36.517 W0°59.745**

Visit by train

To avoid driving and parking in the city, you can visit by train from Balsicas or Torre Pacheco using RENFE or for a picturesque journey from Los Nietos on the shores of the Mar Menor using FEVE. The train station is opposite the main tourist office at the start of the old city walls. The start of our city walking route and the marina are about a 15 minute walk away. Exit the train station and cross the road to the old city wall. Keeping the wall on your left, follow it and you'll arrive at the marina.

Cartagena City Walking Map

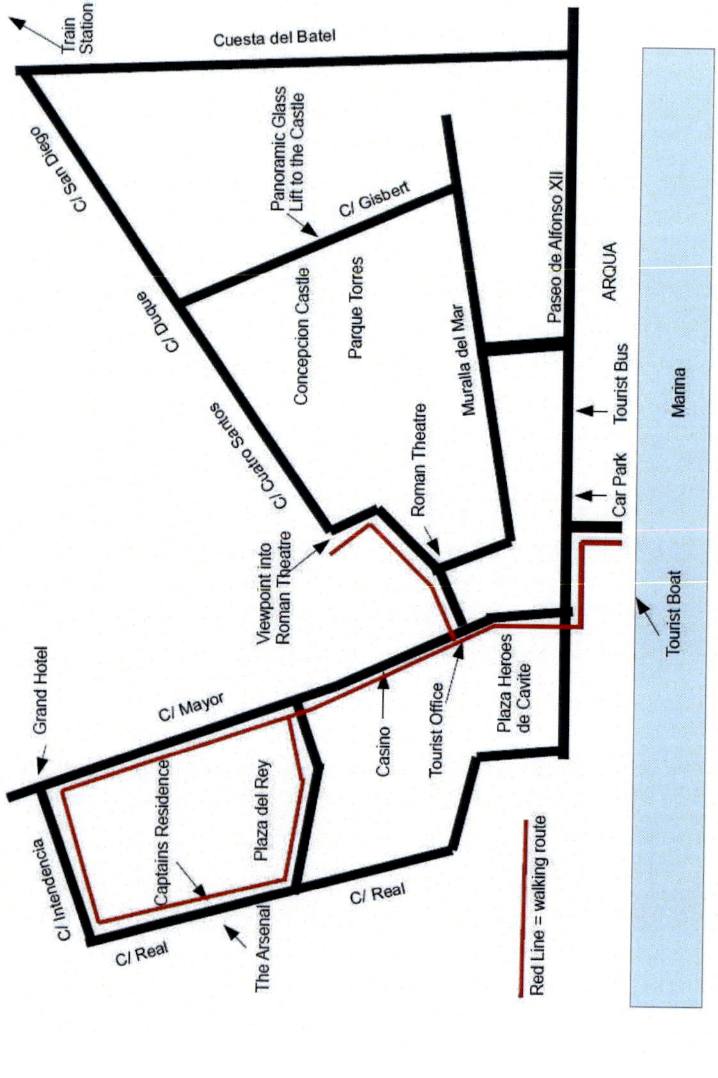

Days Out in Elche City

Elche is also known as the City of Palms as it is located within the largest Palm forest in Europe. This city has two international UNESCO awards; one for its palm groves and the other for its religious play, the Misteri d'Elx which the people of the city have performed annually in August since Medieval times. The week's play is rounded off with one of Spain's loudest firework displays known as the Nit d'Alba.

Once you have visited the Tourist Office, just above the car park, you can explore Elche by following our Elche city walking route. Why not climb the narrow steps up to the roof of the Basilica, from where you get a wonderful view over Elche and its palms. You can visit the various museums including the award winning Archaeological and History Museum or get to know more about the palms at the Huerto del Cura. Stroll through the Municipal Park and go into the Visitors Centre for an audio visual introduction to the city or take the small Tourist Train.

Elche has some great shopping. The large Salvador Artesano shoe factory outlet is a must for all shoe lovers as it is about the size of a football pitch! Nearby is the El Corte Ingles department store. It sells everything that you would expect, is open during siesta and has free parking! The L'Aljub is a large indoor mall with Eroski and many high-street names, plus a Comic Park to keep the Children entertained and free parking!

Visit the Tourist Office for information about the museums and other places of interest. Remember that most museums are closed on a Monday and for siesta which is generally 14.00-16.00 in the winter and 14.00-17.00 in the summer.

Itinerary 1

To get to know the city in one day we suggest starting with a visit to the tourist office to collect a map and more information. Spend the morning following our Elche city walking route to familiarise yourself with the main streets, plazas and buildings. After a relaxing menu del dia take a walk up the bell tower and get a birds eye view of the city with it's many hundreds of palm trees.

Elche Centre Car Park **N38°16.098 W0°41.815**

Parking is in the underground car park beside the municipal park and is charged for by length of stay.

Main Tourist Office

Exit the underground car park, the round white building beside the municipal park is the main tourist office.

Cathedral & Bell Tower

The cathedral was built between 1672 and 1784 and is known as La Basílica Menor de Santa María or Iglesia Arciprestal de Nuestra Señora de la Asunción. It is free to go into the cathedral, but there is an entrance charge to climb the bell tower. The narrow spiral stair case has a number of rooms where you can take a rest, and the views over the city are well worth the effort!

🔗For the most up to date information about opening times and prices take a look at the official link on the website.

Itinerary 2

Spend the morning visiting some of the cities museums like the Archaeological and History Museum, the Misteri d'Elx Museum or the Huerto del Cura with the famous Imperial Palm. Then make the short drive to the eastern side of the city and enjoy an afternoon shopping at the nearby L'Aljub, El Corte Ingles and Salvador Artesano shoe factory.

Elche Centre Car Park N38°16.098 W0°41.815

Parking is in the underground car park beside the municipal park and is charged for by length of stay.

Archaeology & History Museum

The entrance to the museum is on the exit stairs from the car park. The Museo Arqueológico y de Historia de Elche or MAHE for short, is an interactive exhibition about the history of the city.

🔗For the most up to date information about opening times and prices take a look at the official link on the website.

Misteri d'Elx Museum

Located a street away from the cathedral, the museum is all about the world renowned Mystery Play. It has old posters, instruments, singers costumes and a model of the Basilica as well as a half hour audiovisual show which demonstrates the history and emotions that surround this extraordinary performance.

🔗For the most up to date information about opening times and prices take a look at the official link on the website.

Huerto del Cura Museum

The Huerto del Cura, which means the Priests Garden, covers an area of 13,000m2. It is packed with a wide range of Mediterranean and tropical plants including a splendid collection of palms and cacti as well as the impressive 7 branched Imperial Palm.

🔗For the most up to date information about opening times and prices take a look at the official link on the website.

El Corte Ingles Department Store N38°15.474 W0°42.763

Parking is in the underground car park directly below the department store and is free.

L'Aljub Shopping Mall N38°15.727 W0°43.323

Parking is in the car park beside the mall and is free.

🔗 For more information check the official link on the website.

Salvador Artesano Shoe Outlet **N38°15.696 W0°44.068**

Parking is in the car park beside the shop and is free.

For more information check the official link on the website.

Itinerary 3

Take a ride on the little Tourist Train which makes a 40 minute tour of the city. It visits the most important areas including the Municipal Palm Park, the Historic Centre and the Palm Grove Route. Next retrace part of the route and take a wander along the historic high street and the wonderful La Glorieta. Enjoy a leisurely menu del dia and then explore the stunning Municipal Palm Park which has plenty of benches and lots of shade for those hot summer days.

Elche Centre Car Park **N38°16.098 W0°41.815**

Parking is in the underground car park beside the municipal park and is charged for by length of stay.

Tourist Train

This is a 40 minute journey taking in the main places of interest with 5 stops along the way. The tourist train departs from in front of the tourist office beside the Municipal Palm Park.

For the most up to date information, timetables and prices take a look at the official link on the website.

La Glorieta

Exit the city centre car park and follow the city walking route to the La Glorieta Plaza. Situated on the main shopping street, the La Glorieta is widely regarded as the best plaza in Elche, it is always immaculately planted with seasonal blooms and is surrounded by a good selection of bars, cafes and restaurants.

Municipal Palm Park

The entrance to the palm park is just beside the car park. The palm forests were laid out in the 10th century by the Moors. Today there are more than 200,000 palm trees, some of which make up the municipal park. The park has a large children's play area, a dove cote, bandstand, restaurants and free visitors centre.

Elche Football Club

Elche Club de Fútbol is based in Elche. It was founded in 1923, and generally plays in the Spanish La Liga or the Second Division A. It's home ground, called the Estadio Manuel Martinez Valero, has a capacity of 36,000 seats.

🔗For the latest information, fixture list and ticket prices check the official link on the website.

Elche Football Stadium **N38°16.139 W0°40.206**

Visit by train

To avoid driving and parking in the city, you can visit Elche by train from Orihuela or San Isidro (Albatera-Catral). The train station, known as Elche Park or Elx Parc is underground, exit the building and turn left towards the municipal park. Walk through the beautiful Municipal Palm Park towards the tourist office and the cathedral a few minutes away.

Elche City Walking Map

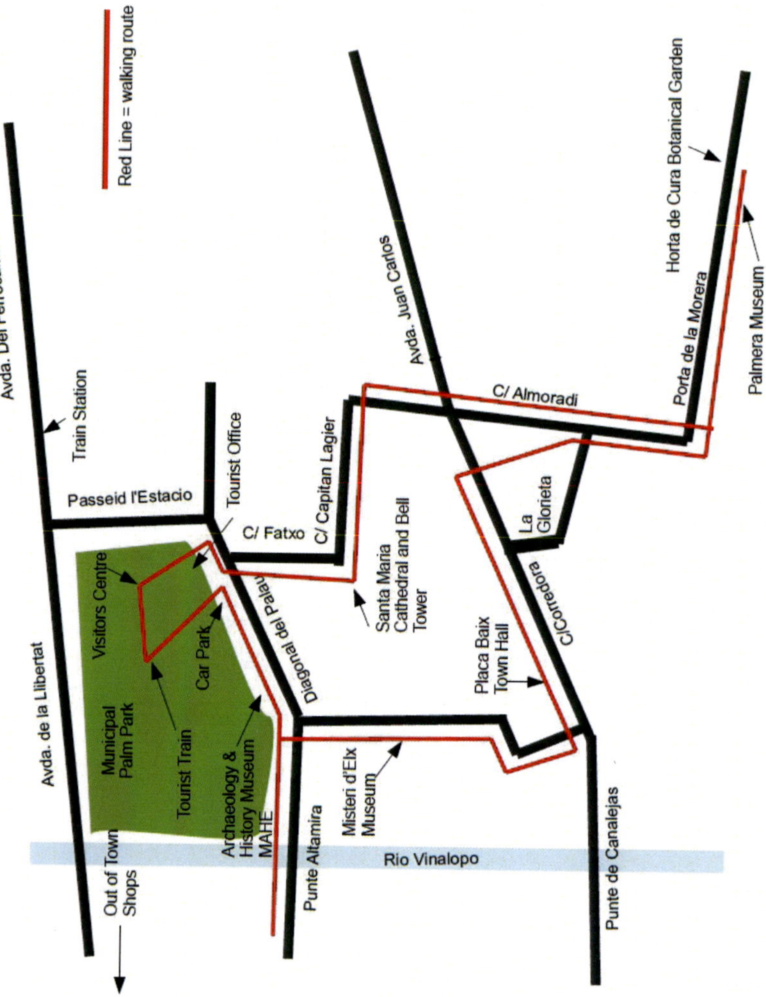

Days Out in Murcia City

The city of Murcia was founded by the Arabs during the 1st century. Since then, it has been a crossroads for different civilizations and core of the Mediterranean as it occupies an important location on the Rio Segura. The impressive Basilica (Cathedral), which sits opposite the modern Tourist Office, makes a great starting point. From here, explore the colourful, lively, little plazas that nestle in between the narrow streets. Murcia has an overwhelming array of museums, art galleries and centres and beautiful historic buildings, so if it is culture that you crave you will certainly enjoy your time here.

Murcia has the largest out of town shopping complex in the area as it consists of two malls and Ikea, not to mention the football stadium of Real Murcia. Parking is free in all car parks, so you can really take your time! The Nueva Condomina mall is set over two floors. It has shops throughout including small boutique-like outlets, whilst outside there are many large stores. The Thader Mall also has two stories of much the same stores and a Ten Pin Bowling Alley. Ikea is just the same as all the other Ikeas! However, apart from weekends, fiestas or rainy days you'll hardly ever bump trolleys!

Visit the Tourist Office for information about the museums and other places of interest. Remember that most museums are closed on a Monday and for siesta which is generally 14.00-16.00 in the winter and 14.00-17.00 in the summer.

Itinerary 1

To get to know the city in one day we suggest starting with a visit to the tourist office to collect a map and more information. Then relax with a coffee in the plaza just outside, and admire the impressive Cathedral before spending some time wandering around inside it. Then follow our Murcia city walking route for a great introduction to the city and its narrow streets and quirky plazas, stopping where you please.

Murcia City Centre Car Park N37°58.977 W1°07.784

Parking: is in the underground car park beside the river and is charged for by length of stay.

Main Tourist Office

Exit the underground car park and facing the town hall turn right and walk along the narrow street , Calle Arenal to the plaza with the modern tourist office and the impressive cathedral.

Cathedral Santa María

Known as the Iglesia Catedral de Santa María in Spanish, it's construction began in 1394 and finished in 1467. It has the tallest bell tower in Spain and 25 bells, all of which were made in the 17th & 18th century. There is no admission charge, but donations are encouraged. It is open in July & August: 07:00-13:00 & 18:00-21:00 and during the rest of the year 07:00-13:00 & 17:00-20:00.

For more information take a look at the official link on the website.

Itinerary 2

Visit some of Murcias many museums, art galleries and churches whilst they are open in the morning, the Casino museum is always a firm favourite. Enjoy lunch and sample some typical Murcian food, then during the afternoon take a stroll beside the river Segura and relax in the botanical garden also known as the Jardin del Malecon

Murcia City Centre Car Park N37°58.977 W1°07.784

Parking: is in the underground car park beside the river and is charged for by length of stay.

Casino Museum

Exit the underground centre car park and follow the walking route to the casino. Constructed in 1847 in the mezda or moorish style, it is quite simply stunning and ultra opulent.

For the most up to date information about opening times and prices take a look at the official link on the website.

Botanical Jardin Malecon Park

The garden was created in 1845 to provide the students of the Natural History and Agriculture College with a space to carry out their practical studies. Since then it has been destroyed twice; once during the war and another time when it became a car park! In the 1970's it was reinstated and since then the work has been on going to improve it.

For more information check the official link on the website.

Itinerary 3

Spend the day at the two massive out of town shopping malls of the Nueva Condomina, the Thader with a multi lane bowling alley and the huge Ikea for some retail therapy. Alternatively you can have a great day out at the Terra Natural Animal and Water Park a couple more junctions south on the A7.

Nueva Condomina Shopping Mall **N38°02.458 W1°08.943**

Parking is in the car park beside the mall and is free. Walk into the massive shopping mall or through the car park to the large individual shops. Remember the Thader mall and Ikea are 2 minutes drive away using the bridge over the motorway.

🔗For more information check the official link on the website.

Thader Ikea Shopping Mall **N38°01.806 W1°08.895**

Parking is in the car park and is free. Walk into the massive shopping mall or cross the car park for Ikea. Remember the Nueva Condomina mall is 2 minutes drive away using the bridge over the motorway.

🔗For more information check the official link on the website.

Terra Natura and Aqua Natura **N38°00.734 W1°09.954**

The Terra Natura Park is divided into two areas; African Savannah and the Iberian Peninsula and has over 300 animals and 50 species of trees and plants. Aqua Natura is a water park and has pools and slides for children and adults as well as a lazy river. Parking is in the car park and there is a fixed charge for the day.

🔗For the most up to date information about opening times and prices take a look at the official link on the website.

Real Murcia Football Club

Real Murcia Club de Fútbol is based in Murcia. It was founded in 1908 and generally plays in the Spanish La Liga or the Second Division, playing home matches at Estadio Nueva Condomina, which can hold 33,045 spectators.

🔗For the latest information, fixture list and ticket prices check the official link on the website.

Murcia Football Stadium **N38°02.458 W1°08.943**

Visit by train

To avoid driving and parking in the city, you can visit Murcia by train. There are two train lines; north to Orihuela, San Isidro (Albatera-Catral), Elche and Alicante, and another east to Balsicas and Cartagena. The train station is a 15 minute walk from the Cathedral and the start of our Murcia city walking route. Leave the train station and continue to the main road Calle Florida Blanca, turn right and go straight over the roundabout. Pass the Jardin Florida Blanca park heading for the river. Cross the Rio Segura river and then turn right towards the Ayuntamiento (town hall).

Murcia City Walking Map

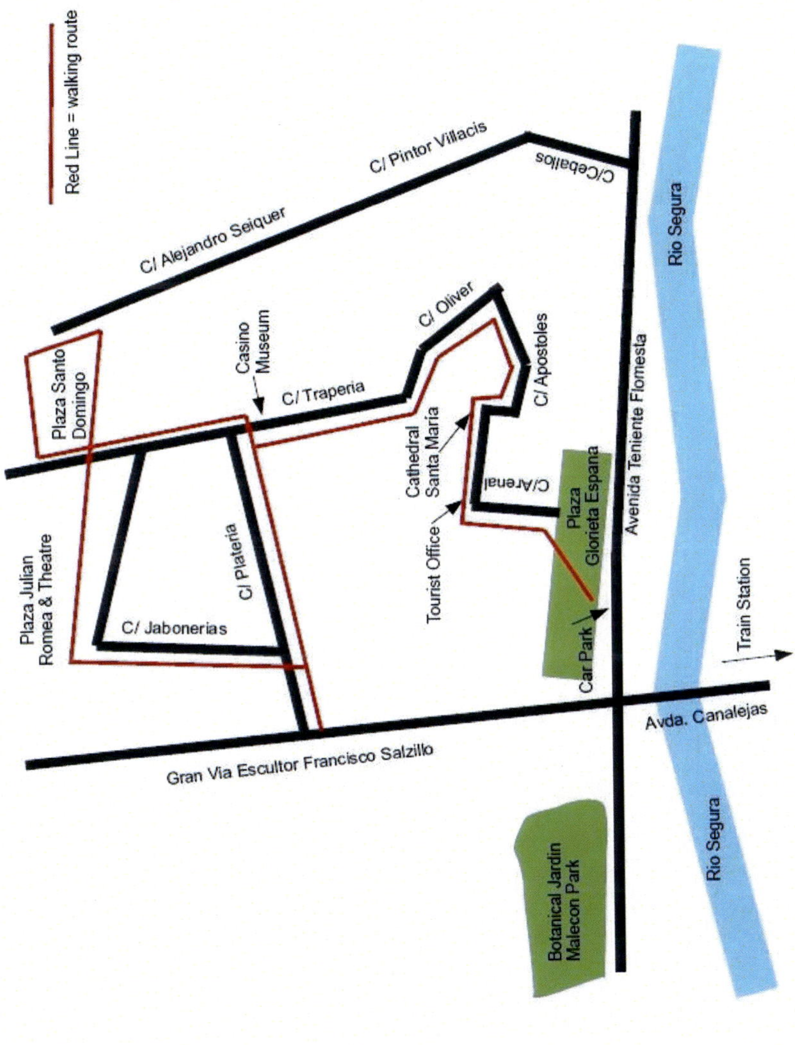